TO

_____

FROM

_____

ON

_____

365 ROMANTIC GIFTS FOR YOUR LOVE

A DAILY GUIDE TO CREATIVE GIVING

365 ROMANTIC GIFTS FOR YOUR LOVE

A DAILY GUIDE TO CREATIVE GIVING

BY TOMIMA EDMARK

THE SUMMIT PUBLISHING GROUP – ARLINGTON, TEXAS

THE SUMMIT PUBLISHING GROUP

One Arlington Centre, 1112 East Copeland Road, Fifth Floor, Arlington, Texas 76011

00 99 98 97   010   5 4 3

Edmark, Tomima L.
365 romantic gifts for your love: a daily guide to creative living/ by Tomima L. Edmark
p. cm.
ISBN 1-56530-211-7 (hardcover: alk. paper)
1. Man-woman relationships--Miscellanea. 2. Love--Miscellanea. 3. Gifts--Miscellanea.
I. Title
HQ801.E34 1996
306.7--dc20

96-13055
CIP

∞ INTRODUCTION ∞

It's a familiar scenario: a holiday or a festive occasion in your Love's life is swiftly approaching, and you want to bestow upon that special someone a special something. You're at the mall; you have a credit card, you have an opportunity...the only thing you don't have is a clue.

What size? What color? What price? What a pain shopping for someone else can be—even when it's for your Love, the person whose presence in your life is worth more than all the presents money can buy. With that in mind, consider spending less time, effort, and money in the pursuit of the perfect present, and channel that energy into giving the perfect gift.

What's the difference between a present and a gift? A present usually goes beside the birthday cake or beneath the holiday tree. It's likely something you give to the recipient because it is something you want them to have. A gift is something you give the recipient that you know they want. You may think it's the dumbest thing, but they want it, so you give it to them.

A gift comes straight from the heart, often without ever having been on a store shelf. A present may be used for awhile then put aside and forgotten, but a gift is cherished by the recipient long after its usefulness has passed. A gift is a memory with a bit of ribbon on it: a parent treasures the lopsided ceramic whatsit created and given by his or her first-grader...even if it was thirty years ago.

"It's the thought that counts" is usually said when someone receives something inappropriate. It's just as easy to put forth the same amount of thought and give a perfect gift. It doesn't matter how much money you spend—it's how much time, effort, and commitment you put into making your gift the most intimate and personal expression of how you feel about your Love.

Still no clue? In this book you'll find 365 creative ideas for special gifts for your Love, many of which require little or no money. Some are frivolous and funny, others are sweet and sentimental; some will impress and amaze, others will charm and delight. It's up to you to pick the gift that will please you as much as it will please your Love.

As you're choosing, remember that the presentation of the gift is a gift in itself. Whenever possible:

- Wrap the gift carefully in attractive paper to increase the elements of surprise and suspense.
- Spend some time decorating the package with ribbons, bows, flowers, or little drawings.
- Include a card or note, even if all it says is "To my Love, from———."
- Make the presentation memorable. Hide it and take your Love on a treasure hunt. Surprise your Love with a gift after a delicious dessert. Offer it on bended knee in a public place.
- Wait until both of you are in a good mood. A gift given after a quarrel or to brighten the blues may be tainted by an unhappy memory, but a gift given in a moment of shared contentment will always bring warm thoughts of that moment.

Why wait for an occasion? The best reason to give a gift is for no reason at all. Make any day a special event with this shopping list from the heart.

∞ 1 ∞

HAPPY HOLIDAY

Make today your Love's special holiday. Give it a name such as "Bill's Golf Day" or "Jane's Pamper Day." Invent unique traditions to be used again next year if you choose to make your Love's holiday an annual event.

∞ 2 ∞

LOVE WRAP

A blanket or hand-made quilt for your Love for those cold nights when you're not available.

∞ 3 ∞

MADE TO ORDER

Send away for catalogs to stores where you know your Love enjoys shopping. Have the catalogs arrive with your Love's pet name appearing on the address label.

∞ 4 ∞

IN THE CARDS

Craft a handmade card to give to your Love. Find a special photo and a meaningful poem or song lyric that creates a special message to your Love. Add a splash of your cologne or perfume before sealing it with a kiss.

∞ 5 ∞

WINDOW WITH A VIEW

Build or buy a wooden flower box. Fill it with flowers or herbs and install it outside the window most used by your Love.

∞ 6 ∞

FOR ALL YOU DO...

This bud's for you. One very special flower chosen by you and presented in a unique bud vase.

∞ 7 ∞

PET SMART
A gift for your Love's prized pet.

∞ 8 ∞

JUST FOR FUN
A coloring book with a set of crayons or watercolor markers.
For fun, color in one of the pages and sign it.

∞ 9 ∞

CHANNEL SURFER
Your remote control with a big ribbon around it and a note
attached, giving either hours you promise not to watch TV or
giving hours for your Love to watch TV uninterrupted.

∞ 10 ∞

WHITE ELEPHANT
Repair, paint, or reupholster that item your Love has been
meaning to fix up but hasn't had the time to do.

∞ 11 ∞

HOME CARD SHOP
Give your Love a bundle of greeting cards to use when there isn't time to shop for any. Buy a selection for several occasions.

∞ 12 ∞

OLDIES BUT GOODIES
Convert all your Love's eight-millimeter home movies to videocassettes.

∞ 13 ∞

TREE OF LIFE
Research your Love's family and formulate their family tree.

∞ 14 ∞

STORMY WEATHER
A pair of rain boots for your Love which you have customized with craft paint.

∞ 15 ∞

IN THE HAT

Write down the name of each restaurant your Love enjoys on separate sheets of paper, then put them in a hat. Your gift is letting your Love go to the hat once a month and select a restaurant for dinner.

∞ 16 ∞

THE ENVELOPE, PLEASE

Did you know it is easy to make your own envelope? Simply pull apart a basic envelope, trace the shape onto some fun paper (e.g. the funnies, yellow pages, legal brief), and then paste the edges. Write a note, put it inside, and mail it to your Love.

∞ 17 ∞

IN THE SPIRIT

A share of stock in the vineyard or brewery of your Love's favorite wine or beer.

☜ 18 ☞

ONE DOZEN WAYS

Select twelve freshly cut flowers and put each one in a special place. For example, on your Love's pillow, in the cereal bowl, on the car seat, in shoes, inside the shower, on top of the television...

☜ 19 ☞

SPECIAL MEMBER

A membership to a book club, video club, or software club.

☜ 20 ☞

ADDITIONAL READING

A subscription to a magazine you know your Love would like.

☜ 21 ☞

TAKING LICENSE

Buy a personalized license plate for your Love's car.

∞ 22 ∞

BEHIND CLOSED DOORS

Empty one of your Love's closets, then refill it with balloons.
Once the door is opened and the balloon shower is over, a
sentimental sign on the wall of the closet is revealed. For
example, "My love for you inflates every day."

∞ 23 ∞

OUT ON A LIMB

A five-gallon tree with a big bow tied around it. Agree upon
where this "always growing" symbol of your affection for your
Love should be planted. Promise to carve both of your initials
in it when it becomes large enough. (Warning: If you have a
brown thumb, this gift is not for you. It's bad karma if this
symbolic gift should start to die.)

∞ 24 ∞

CHARMING

A charm engraved with the first phone number you used to
call your Love and the date of the phone call.

∞ 25 ∞

LOCK IT UP

Find a fun-looking lock and key. Paint them gold and, if possible, decorate. Give it to your Love with the note: "You now have control of my heart."

∞ 26 ∞

HALF IS BETTER THAN THE WHOLE

Find some object symbolic of the two of you (heart, coin, key, stone, bolt) and have it cut in half to make his-and-her key chains.

∞ 27 ∞

ACROSS & DOWN

Create a crossword puzzle using your relationship as the theme for the clues. Make your clues funny and sentimental. Be available if your Love needs help with the answers.

❦ 28 ❦

THE FUNNIES

Pick out a comic strip and paste your own captions over the existing ones.

❦ 29 ❦

ARTIFACTS

Select meaningful things sitting around the house, in drawers, up in the attic, down in the basement, and give them a new home in some beautiful box.

❦ 30 ❦

SUITABLE FOR FRAMING

Find something special to be framed. It can be the ticket stubs to your first movie together, a napkin or menu from your Love's favorite restaurant, or one of your Love's sayings handwritten in calligraphy. Use your imagination.

∞ 31 ∞

CRYSTAL BALL

Have a fortune teller predict your Love's future. Note: Make
sure it will be positive.

∞ 32 ∞

GET-WELL KIT

The next time your Love is sick, buy everything on the
drugstore shelf that might help your Love get well sooner.
Include a get-well card, favorite candy, an ice or heat pack,
and magazines your Love would like. Assemble it all in a
basket and deliver it personally.

∞ 33 ∞

BRIGHT SMILES

A new set of toothbrushes for the two of you with a different
flavor of toothpaste than you normally use.

∞ 34 ∞

PERSONAL SACRIFICE

That favorite shirt, socks, shoes, or hat your Love wishes
you'd throw away: Wrap it up and give it to your Love to do
with as your Love wishes. This is the ultimate sign of
compromise.

∞ 35 ∞

CARE PACKAGE

Mail or have delivered a care package to your Love at work.
Include your Love's favorite foods, music with a player,
flowers, pillow, poem, and, of course, a sentimental card.

∞ 36 ∞

SPECIAL KEY

Search for a key that is special to you, and give it to your
Love as the "key to your heart" to put on your Love's key
chain. You might even engrave a special message on it.

∾ 37 ∾

LUNAR EXPERIENCE

Give your Love a moon…specifically, yours. Add to your
Love's surprise by strategically placing on your "moon" a
temporary tattoo.

∾ 38 ∾

FAVORITE SONG

Locate the sheet music or have the lyrics written out to your
Love's favorite song, or the music you danced to at your
wedding. You might even have it framed.

∾ 39 ∾

MORNING PREP

Observe your Love's morning routine. The next evening lay
out your Love's clothes, put toothpaste on the brush, arrange
shaving/cosmetic accessories, get out hair-related items, and
anything else you can think of to speed up your Love's
morning routine. You might even begin with breakfast in bed.

∞ 40 ∞

SPECIAL HAIR
Give your Love a lock of your hair to be carried in a wallet.

∞ 41 ∞

BETWEEN THE SHEETS
Spray your Love's sheets with perfume or cologne for a
"scent"-imental evening.

∞ 42 ∞

CANDY ALTERNATIVE
If your Love shouldn't or doesn't want to eat candy, here is a
healthy alternative. Give your Love a candy box filled with
golf balls, CDs, stationery, jewelry, or dried fruit.

∞ 43 ∞

SPONGY
A beautiful sponge with a note offering to wash your Love's
back any time.

∞ 44 ∞

BOOK AND BALLS

Give your Love three balls and a book (or video) on juggling.
Offer to help your Love learn this new skill.

∞ 45 ∞

ANONYMOUS NOTE

Send an unsigned note to your Love explaining that a present
is waiting at a certain location and time, and the name of the
person to contact to receive the gift. Some suggestions would
be a cigar at a tobacco shop, lingerie at a lingerie store, tie at
a men's shop, a gift certificate to the store you have sent your
Love to.

∞ 46 ∞

HOT WRAP

While your Love is in the shower, sneak the towel away and
warm it up in the dryer for a few minutes, then put it back
where you found it.

∞ 47 ∞

BAR OF SOAP

Carve your Love's initials or a special message onto a
beautiful bar of soap.

∞ 48 ∞

PERSONAL CHECK

Make out a check to your Love for one million kisses. When
your Love endorses it, be prepared to pucker up.

∞ 49 ∞

BATHROOM SINK

Fill the sink with water, then float flowers, rubber ducks,
boats, or anything else you can think of.

∞ 50 ∞

DIMMER

Install a light dimmer on the bathroom or bedroom light
switch.

∞ 51 ∞

PREFERRED POWDER

Send an envelope to your Love containing a favorite powder. Some suggestions might be bath salts, instant coffee, hot chocolate mix, citrus drink mix, foot powder, or talcum powder.

∞ 52 ∞

JUST DOUGH IT

Buy or make the dough for your Love's favorite cookies and present it. Your Love now has the choice of either eating it raw or saving it to cook whenever a cookie is desired. Remember to write down the baking instructions.

∞ 53 ∞

WILDLIFE

The Wolf Education and Research Center in Ketchum, Idaho, will let you pick and adopt a wolf for only $25. Call (208) 726-2860.

∽ 54 ∾

TEN

Buy ten lipsticks or shaving creams for your Love to try for a change in routine.

∽ 55 ∾

SOUND THE BELLS

A pair of bells with a note saying, "These bells will remind me never to let you become a distant sound."

∽ 56 ∾

PRIVACY, PLEASE

Make or buy a "Do Not Disturb" sign for your Love to hang on a door knob.

∽ 57 ∾

PERSONAL STAR

Name a star after your Love with the Star Registry in Ingleside, Illinois. Call (847) 546-5533.

❧ 58 ❧

ORNAMENTAL GIFTS

Collect meaningful little objects throughout the year, or make cards with special thoughts. Turn them into Christmas tree ornaments to give to your Love on the day the two of you put up the tree. Even one special memento or thought is still great.

❧ 59 ❧

REACH OUT AND TOUCH

Write a note promising to touch your Love affectionately every day, even if you might be upset with them. Begin with a kiss after your Love has read the note.

❧ 60 ❧

POM-POMS

A pair of cheerleader pom-poms and a note attached which reads, "I'll always be your head cheerleader."

◌ 61 ◌

CHEERY CHERRIES

A bowl of cherries and a note that reads, "Life with you is a bowl of cherries."

◌ 62 ◌

YARD SIGN

Make a sign like you see sprouting in people's yards during elections. However, your sign is a vote for your Love. Something like, "My vote goes to (Love's name) for treasurer of my affections." Now put it in your yard as a surprise.

◌ 63 ◌

SAY CHEESE!

Secretly have a picture taken of yourself. Make a 5"x7" print and put it in a frame for your Love's office. Also have a small print made to put in your Love's wallet.

∞ 64 ∞

KISSLETOE

Give your Love a dried sprig of mistletoe and proclaim that it's good all year for a kiss from you, any time. Wrap it in a pouch so your Love can carry it easily in a pocket or purse.

∞ 65 ∞

LOVE STAMP

Find a company that makes rubber stamps and have a personalized one made up for your Love. It could be an actual reproduction of your lip print, a heart shape with both of your initials inside, the loving nickname you use when referring to your Love, or anything else special. Don't forget to include a red ink pad.

∞ 66 ∞

NUTS TO YOU

A jar of your Love's favorite nuts. Of course, a note inside reads, "I'm absolutely nuts about you."

∞ 67 ∞

FOR SALE SIGN

A sign in the shape of a heart with "For Sale" written on it, and "Sold" stamped through it. Place it out in front of your house or on the front door.

∞ 68 ∞

REFRIGERATOR ACCESSORY

Locate a poem, cartoon, or saying that you know your Love will enjoy. Have it sealed in plastic and attach a magnet on the back. Put it on the refrigerator for your Love to find.

∞ 69 ∞

SIGN IT

Dream up a message you want to give your Love, then print it out on several signs for your Love to read while driving up the driveway, like the old Burma Shave ads.

∞ 70 ∞

COOKIES WITH A HEART

Bake your Love heart-shaped cookies decorated with special messages.

∞ 71 ∞

THE WRITE STUFF

Write your Love a romantic story. After your Love reads it, act out the love scenes.

∞ 72 ∞

LEFTY

Is your Love lefthanded? Make a present of the *Lefthander Magazine*. Write to P.O. Box 8249, Topeka, KS, 66608

∞ 73 ∞

COOKING IN STYLE

Find a kitchen or barbecue utensil you think would make your Love's cooking life a little easier.

∞ 74 ∞

FIERY SCENT

Make scented candles using fragrances you know your Love
will like. Put them in the bedroom or bathroom.

∞ 75 ∞

FLOWER POWER

Hire a floral arranger to come to your Love's home and
decorate the bedroom and bed with fresh cut flowers.

∞ 76 ∞

A PRIVATE TABLE FOR TWO

Perform a table dance for your Love at home. Have music
playing and clothing flying.

∞ 77 ∞

A TOUCH OF CLASS

Buy your Love a pair of opera gloves and two tickets to the
opera.

∞ 78 ∞

FRIDGE FUN

Surprise your Love by making chocolate pudding, topping it with whipped cream. Have it waiting the next time your Love opens the refrigerator.

∞ 79 ∞

A GOOD OLD TIME

Rent the movie "Two for the Road," starring Albert Finney and Audrey Hepburn, and watch it together barefoot with a big bowl of popcorn.

∞ 80 ∞

BACK TO BASICS

Give the gift of a backrub to your Love in private. If you don't give it, hire a masseuse to come to your home. Perform the rub in the evening so there can be candles and soft music.

∞ 81 ∞

STARTERS AND HAPPY ENDINGS

Take your Love to a favorite restaurant. Order only appetizers and desserts. Share everything ordered with each other.

∞ 82 ∞

HAIR RAISING

Arrange an appointment for your Love to get a haircut at a very fancy salon.

∞ 83 ∞

SOFT-TO-WARE

Go shopping for some software for your Love's computer. There are some great screen savers on the market.

∞ 84 ∞

PROPELLER HEAD

Buy your Love a beanie with a propeller on top.

∞ 85 ∞

PHOTO FINISH

Gather up all your Love's loose photos and organize them. If you know your Love would be picky about the way this is done, go out and buy all the equipment to make this possible, then sit down with your Love and organize them together.

∞ 86 ∞

OVER-CREDITED

Decide you have too many credit cards. Give the ones you will no longer use to your Love to destroy. Have a meltdown or cutting ceremony.

∞ 87 ∞

THE GOOD OLD DAYS

Find a special memento to give from your Love's hometown. It could be a T-shirt from your Love's alma mater, a picture of the hospital where your Love was born, or a mug with the town's name on it. Be creative, and the gift will be very special.

∞ 88 ∞

RACY REFRIGERATOR

Replace the light bulb inside your Love's refrigerator with a colored one.

∞ 89 ∞

BOX IT UP

Buy a kid's lunch box you know your Love would like. Fill it with some favorite snacks so your Love will always have something to munch on at work. If you can find your Love's childhood lunch box, all the better.

∞ 90 ∞

FOR KEEPS

Make your Love a keepsake box. Decoupage photos, ticket stubs, greeting cards, business cards, and other meaningful items on it. Give the box to your Love with a big ribbon tied around it.

∞ 91 ∞

HAND CONTROL

Give your Love a hand puppet and explain that it is a whipping boy. Your Love is to use it to vent anger at someone. You may want to include a mini whip as an accessory.

∞ 92 ∞

IT'S A WASH

Have a shiny, clean car waiting for your Love with a love note attached to the steering wheel or stick shift. Leave a lip print on the rearview mirror.

∞ 93 ∞

MINI VACATION

Give a certificate to your Love good for a thirty-minute break or vacation whenever your Love feels the need. You finish whatever task your Love was doing before cashing in the certificate.

∞ 94 ∞

NECKING AND PETTING

Buy a new collar for your Love's pet with its custom name tag already made and attached.

∞ 95 ∞

FROZEN TO PERFECTION

Make ice cubes that have flower petals, fruit, candy, or something else your Love likes frozen in the middle. Put them in your Love's freezer for a surprising discovery.

∞ 96 ∞

HOT PACK

A box of matches, thermometer, Tabasco sauce, postcard from the Caribbean, picture of the sun, chili pepper, candle, and fireball candy. Put them all in a box with a note at the bottom which reads: "I'm Hot for You!"

∞ 97 ∞

DEFINITELY WANTED

Make a "Most Wanted" poster of your Love. For example:
"Wanted:_____ for stealing my heart. Last seen driving a _____
headed toward _____. Reward: Eternal Love. Signed,
Sheriff _____."

∞ 98 ∞

TRULY FRUITY

A fruit basket for your Love, but with a twist: Write messages
on the fruit. For example, "top banana," "the orange-inal,"
"my peach," "applicious."

∞ 99 ∞

A TISKET, A TASKET

Put together a basket of all the foods your Love adores. If
your Love is following a diet, find interesting foods that can
be eaten without cheating.

∞ 100 ∞

ASTROLOGICAL INFLUENCE
Write your Love an original horoscope for the day.

∞ 101 ∞

TWO TICKETS TO PARADISE
Two tickets to a sporting, cultural, musical, or entertainment event your Love would like to attend. Either go yourself or graciously offer to let your Love take a friend.

∞ 102 ∞

OUT THE KAZOO
Buy a pair of kazoos for the two of you.

∞ 103 ∞

PET FOR YOUR PET
Has your Love always wanted a pet? Make that wish come true.

∞ 104 ∞

GOOD LUCK

Surprise your Love by buying lottery tickets that have special numbers such as your Love's birthday, phone number, address, date of your first meeting, etc. Buy as many tickets as you can come up with numbers for.

∞ 105 ∞

BIRTH BOOK

Go to the library and find as many newspapers as you can with the date of your Love's birthday. Compile a notebook or collage of all the special events of the day and give it to your Love.

∞ 106 ∞

FLOWER POWER

Bring home a corsage or boutonniere for your Love to wear to work or church.

∞ 107 ∞

LOVING CUP

Make a customized coffee cup for your Love by finding one of the many places that sell "green" ceramic pieces and then customizing it with glazes.

∞ 108 ∞

CUSTOM WALKERS

Sneak away with your Love's favorite pair of athletic shoes and give them a personal touch. First clean them up, then buy fun new laces. Draw characters on them, or even dye them. Present them wrapped in a shoe box.

∞ 109 ∞

A GREAT SHOWER

Does your Love's shower head drizzle instead of spray? Does your Love have regular old soap instead of a nice scented one? Could your Love use a new shower caddie? Buy your Love all the items necessary to turn his or her shower into a sanctuary.

∞ 110 ∞

UP AND OVER

Treat your Love to a makeup or makeover. If you can't afford
a fancy spa, solicit friends to help, or offer to barter for
services. Note: Men need makeovers, too.

∞ 111 ∞

SPECIAL NOTE

Cut a musical note out of construction paper and have it
sealed in acrylic to have your Love use as a paperweight.
Explain to your Love that it is an eternal love note.

∞ 112 ∞

CREATURE COMFORTS

Buy or build your Love a birdhouse, hummingbird feeder,
birdbath, or whatever will attract favorite creatures to your
Love's home.

∞ 113 ∞

AUTO ENTERTAINMENT

Does your Love commute to work? Find something that will
help make the commute less painful. It could be an
audiobook, a music or exercise cassette, a pillow to sit on, or
whatever.

∞ 114 ∞

TIME FOR A HUG

Put a big bow on one of your Love's chairs. Explain it is a
"timeout" chair. When your Love sits in it, you know you need
to go over and give that special person a big hug and kiss.

∞ 115 ∞

IN SEASON

Go to the local public market and buy your Love's favorite
fruits or vegetables that are in season. Lovingly pick each
piece, making sure every one is just right.

∞ 116 ∞

HEAD GEAR

Find a special hat to protect your Love when enjoying a favorite outdoor activity such as walking, golfing, gardening, or fishing.

∞ 117 ∞

FRAME-UP

Find all the reasons your Love is special to you in words found in magazines. Now, on a piece of special paper write: "I cherish you because…" and fill the paper with all the reasons. Now, frame your work.

∞ 118 ∞

CUSTOM FIT

Create custom gift certificates of things tailored to your Love. For example, a round of golf at a favorite course, a day of beauty at a salon, a week of carpool.

❦ 119 ❦

HANG-UPS

Hang those pictures or items your Love has been meaning to
hang on the wall but has never had time to do.

❦ 120 ❦

MIX IT UP

Oil and vinegar may not mix, but they are still popular on
salads. Shop the market for a very special bottle of virgin oil
and an unusual vinegar to give to your Love.

❦ 121 ❦

TIME CAPSULE

Find a container to turn into a time capsule. Fill it with
things that have special meaning to your relationship. Give it
to your Love with the understanding that each anniversary
the two of you will review its contents and add meaningful
new items.

∽ 122 ∾

WIPE IT UP
Buy a new set of wiper blades for your Love's car.

∽ 123 ∾

LUBE JOB
Surprise your Love by having the oil changed in your Love's car. While you're at it, how about filling the windshield washer and checking the transmission fluid?

∽ 124 ∾

LOVE SHIELD
Write a sweet love note to your Love and deliver it by putting it under the wiper blade of the car's windshield.

∽ 125 ∾

TAKE IT OUT
Bring home your Love's favorite Chinese food as a surprise.

∞ 126 ∞

PAPER THAT'S PERSONAL

Go through today's newspaper before your Love does. Draw mustaches on all the photos, write editorial comments in the margins, underline interesting facts, and highlight articles you think your Love would like to read. Give this personalized edition for your Love's personal enjoyment.

∞ 127 ∞

A GREAT PERCENTAGE

Make a sign with a big 100 percent symbol on it. In a note, tell your Love this sign is a symbol of your commitment to the relationship. If you're really bold and committed, put 200 percent instead.

∞ 128 ∞

IT'S THE DETAILS THAT COUNT

Have your Love's car detailed.

∞ 129 ∞

AWARD WINNER

Go to a trophy store and buy a trophy, blue ribbon, plaque, medal, or whatever. Have it personalized with "World's Best Love," "First Place Partner," "Olympic Spouse," or a special award you come up with that you believe would honor your love. Perform an awards ceremony in your Love's honor.

∞ 130 ∞

LOVE COUPONS

Design and make a collection of coupons for your Love to redeem at any time. Some ideas: a car wash and wax, two loads of laundry, a day of "taxi" service, garbage take-out, errand runner for a day.

∞ 131 ∞

SHINING EXAMPLES

Go through your Love's collection of shoes and shine the ones that need shining. You can take this gift a step further and take care of any shoes needing repair.

∞ 132 ∞

NUMBERS GAME

Count up the number of days you and your Love have been together. Count out that number in beans, toothpicks, pennies or anything else you want and put them in a jar with a note of explanation.

∞ 133 ∞

FAST GIFT

Buy a book of gift certificates to your Love's favorite fast-food restaurant.

∞ 134 ∞

CLOSE SHAVE

Buy your Love a new shaver and razor blades. Better yet, put together a "shaving kit" made up of shaving items you think your Love might like to try.

∞ 135 ∞

ORNAMENTAL PLEASURE
Find a very special Christmas tree ornament for your Love.

∞ 136 ∞

PIT STOP
Fill your Love's car with gas.

∞ 137 ∞

TOY STORY
What was your Love's favorite toy as a child? Find out. Then find it, or one like it, and give it to your Love.

∞ 138 ∞

LETTER PERFECT
Find some very special stationery for your Love and have it personalized with your Love's name and address.

∞ 139 ∞

FAVORITE EATERY

Get the menu from your Love's favorite restaurant. Wrap a
bow around it and attach a card with the date and time of
your reservation.

∞ 140 ∞

SPECIAL SLICES

A loaf of unusual bread, freshly baked. Include a special
spread to go with it.

∞ 141 ∞

BOTTLE OF MEMORIES

The next time the two of you celebrate with a bottle of wine
or champagne, keep the cork, remove the label from the
bottle, put them in a pretty box with the date and reason for
the celebration written on the top, and give it to your Love.
This could be the beginning of a collection.

∞ 142 ∞

STACKING THE DECK

A deck of cards to be used for a game of strip poker when both of you are in the mood.

∞ 143 ∞

HOMEMADE, HOMEMADE

Whatever it takes, make (not buy) your Love's favorite dessert.

∞ 144 ∞

PRERECORDED

Videotape a television show you know your Love would like to see but for whatever reason usually can't.

∞ 145 ∞

AN OLD FAVORITE

That favorite shirt, dress, or sweater your Love won't get rid of but never wears? Have a pillow made out of it.

∞ 146 ∞

BY CANDLELIGHT

Have a candle at the ready for a candlelight meal the next
time the two of you go to a fast-food restaurant. If you order
at the drive-through and eat in the car, prop the candle in
the ashtray.

∞ 147 ∞

WHEN IT HAS TO GET THERE

Send your Love a card, poem, or note using one of the
overnight delivery services or a special courier. Call it "Love
Express."

∞ 148 ∞

FIRST MOMENTS

Remember the first time you met your Love? Collect
memorabilia from that moment and make a collage.
Memorabilia could include a matchbook or menu from the
restaurant, a business card from the friend who set you up, or
the page from your calendar with that date.

∽ 149 ∽

FAMILY INTERVIEW

Interview family members about your Love. Ask them to comment on all the wonderful things your Love did while growing up. Write up a report and give it to your Love in a binder.

∽ 150 ∽

TICKTOCK

A clock that is set to the time zone of one of your Love's family members or a dear friend who doesn't live nearby.

∽ 151 ∽

HANDKERCHIEF

Handkerchiefs are such wonderful items, and no one seems to carry them anymore. Buy some for your Love and have them monogrammed.

∽ 152 ∽

THIS OLD HOUSE

Give your Love a framed series of photographs showing every house and/or apartment building your Love has ever lived in.

∽ 153 ∽

FAMILY OF PRODUCTS

Buy all the ancillary products to your Love's favorite fragrance, such as the body lotion, bath gel, soap, aftershave, etc.

∽ 154 ∽

ALMA MATER

A collection of items from every school your Love attended. If possible, see if you can find something from your Love's nursery and grade school. Check with the schools. Most of them are now selling T-shirts and hats with the school's name on them. If not, go to a store that customizes things and have the school name put on it.

∽ 155 ∽

ACTOR/ACTRESS

Buy or rent a movie starring your Love's favorite actor or actress, to watch with or without you (give your Love the option). If you can find it, also bring home a poster of the star.

∽ 156 ∽

TOP-TEN LIST

A top-ten list of reasons why you love your Love.

∽ 157 ∽

IN THE STARS

Have an astrological chart done on your Love.

∽ 158 ∽

HEAVENLY SOUNDS

Hire a harpist to play for your Love during a romantic meal at home.

∽ 159 ∾

NAME & ADDRESS
Take your Love's current address book with all the crossouts and additions and rewrite it into a new book.

∽ 160 ∾

MARKING THE SPOT
Craft a special bookmark for your Love and present it between the pages of a book you know your Love would enjoy reading.

∽ 161 ∾

IF YOU WATER IT, IT WILL GROW
A plant for your Love's office or for a special room at home. Include in the note that you'll be taking care of it.

∽ 162 ∾

GO FLY...
Buy your Love a kite and string.

∞ 163 ∞

PERFECT TOAST

Buy two very special glasses to be used by only the two of you on special occasions.

∞ 164 ∞

FUNNY VALENTINE

Make a valentine and give it to your Love any day but February 14.

∞ 165 ∞

LIGHTS. CAMERA?

A set of red light bulbs.

∞ 166 ∞

HANGING ON

Look in your Love's closet and notice what type of hangers are in short supply. Now, go buy your Love a dozen of that kind.

∞ 167 ∞

SORT IT OUT
Sort out the green M&Ms from a bag you've bought, then
put them in a box or jar to be given to your Love.

∞ 168 ∞

BURNIN' UP
Bring home firewood and anything else necessary to make a
fire.

∞ 169 ∞

HUGS & KISSES
A bag each of Hershey's® Hugs and Kisses with a "Thinking-
of-You" note attached.

∞ 170 ∞

PIECE OF CAKE
Have a bakery make an "I Love You" cake in your Love's
favorite flavor.

∞ 171 ∞

INFLATABLY YOURS

Buy a package of balloons and write "I Love You" on each one. Don't blow them up, but rather place them in a pretty box to give to your Love.

∞ 172 ∞

POETIC SENTIMENT

Find a love poem that expresses the special feelings you have for your Love. Locate a calligrapher to write it up for you, then put it in a frame.

∞ 173 ∞

IT'S PERSONAL

Record a cassette of personal thoughts you want to share with your Love. Perhaps singing (even if off-key) a song that has a special meaning will get your feelings across.

∞ 174 ∞

COOKIE MONSTER

Find a bakery that will make a cookie the size of a pizza.
Have a special message written on it in icing.

∞ 175 ∞

"HEART"-Y

A heart-shaped box filled with your Love's favorite hard
candy.

∞ 176 ∞

GOOD VIBRATIONS

Select one of the many massage gadgets currently on the
market and attach a note promising to use it on your Love
whenever desired.

∞ 177 ∞

SIX-PACK

Present your Love with a favorite beverage in a six-pack.

∞ 178 ∞

BATHE IN LUXURY

Soap, bubble bath, sponges, rubber ducky, or whatever. Put together all the paraphernalia for a wonderful bath. Offer to draw the water and wash your Love's back.

∞ 179 ∞

POETRY IN MOTION

Write a poem to your Love. It's all right to plagiarize from works by the experts as long as you change it enough to make it personal. Make sure it looks suitable for framing…it just might end up that way.

∞ 180 ∞

IT'S A POP

Whether it's gourmet or the good old-fashioned kind, buy some popcorn to share while snuggling together in front of the TV.

∞ 181 ∞

A TEE

Find a T-shirt to give your Love which has something special
written on it.

∞ 182 ∞

COOL WHIP

A beautifully wrapped can of whipped cream. What it goes
on is up to your Love....

∞ 183 ∞

BOBBING BOBBLE

A love note rolled up inside a corked bottle bobbing in a
bath you've drawn for your Love.

∞ 184 ∞

CREATE A LATHER

Some beautiful, expensive, fragrant soap.

∞ 185 ∞

TRUE FORTUNE

Did you know it's possible to buy fortune cookies with personalized fortunes placed inside? Find out who does this in your area.

∞ 186 ∞

LETTER OF AMORE

We are not talking card or note here. Sit down and write a full-blown lovey, gooey-sweet love letter to your Love with all the feelings and sentiments you can muster.

∞ 187 ∞

WASH IT OUT OF YOUR HAIR

Shampoo and conditioner selected specifically for your Love's hair type, with a handmade coupon attached good for one free shampooing performed by you.

∞ 188 ∞

WRITING TO BE READ
Scour a bookstore to find a book or books you know your
Love would like.

∞ 189 ∞

SIGNED, SEALED, DELIVERED
Send a card or note to your Love's parents, thanking them for
creating such a wonderful human being.

∞ 190 ∞

SPECIAL DELIVERY
Make arrangements to have lunch delivered to your Love at
work or home.

∞ 191 ∞

TIMEOUT
Hire a babysitter to take care of the kids as a surprise. Let
your Love decide whether to go out or just stay home.

∞ 192 ∞

SPECIAL SCENT

For no good reason, surprise your Love with a gift of favorite perfume or cologne. If you know your Love has enough of it, consider body lotion or soap in the same scent.

∞ 193 ∞

A.M. SURPRISE

Present your Love with all the fixings for a favorite breakfast. Offer to make it for your Love tomorrow morning. Even serve it in bed, if requested.

∞ 194 ∞

BULK MAIL

Spend time selecting ten sentimental cards to send to your Love. Buy "Love" postage stamps, then send them all on the same day.

∞ 195 ∞

POP SECRET
An inflated balloon with a hidden love note and confetti inside. Present it to your Love with a pin.

∞ 196 ∞

ANTS NOT INCLUDED
Put together a picnic of all the foods your Love loves. Present it in a pretty basket wrapped in a blanket.

∞ 197 ∞

HEAD REST
Surprise your Love with a new pillow to sleep on. Make sure you did your homework to know preferences and possible allergies.

∞ 198 ∞

SWEETS FOR THE SWEET
A box, jar, or basket of your Love's favorite candy.

∞ 199 ∞

ADMIT TWO

Most movie theaters will let you buy advance tickets for a show. Surprise your Love with two tickets to a movie your Love wants to see.

∞ 200 ∞

TAKING A TOLL

A roll of coins or tokens for your Love to use on toll roads and bridges.

∞ 201 ∞

NEW FLAME

A beautiful set of tapered candles to be set on the table for a romantic candlelight dinner for two.

∞ 202 ∞

CHARITABLE CONTRIBUTION

A surprise donation to your Love's favorite charity.

⟣ 203 ⟢

LUCKY NUMBERS

Give your Love ten lottery tickets. If possible, get the tickets from the lottery in your Love's home state.

⟣ 204 ⟢

A FEW FAVORITE THINGS

Prepare or buy your Love's favorite food. Of course, making a favorite (even if not as good) is always more special.

⟣ 205 ⟢

WORK IT OUT

Give your Love a workout. Buy admission to an aerobics class, and the two of you go together.

⟣ 206 ⟢

MUSIC TO THE EARS

Music is always a very special gift. Buy a CD or tape by an artist you know your Love adores.

∞ 207 ∞

PUT IT IN WRITING

Your Love can never have enough pens or pencils. Discover
your Love's favorite kind and buy one. If it's a pen, make sure
you get your Love's preferred ink color.

∞ 208 ∞

CUP RUNNETH OVER

What is your Love's favorite beverage? Coffee? Tea? Wine?
Beer? Whatever it is, present it gift-wrapped with the
appropriate mixers, condiments, and glasses.

∞ 209 ∞

PERIODICALLY

Your Love will always appreciate the gift of favorite
periodicals. It could be your Love's hometown paper, fashion
or car magazines, comic books, or gossip rags.

∞ 210 ∞

UPDATED AND UP-TO-SPEED

If your Love travels, next time your Love is gone, record on
the VCR interesting news segments and shows you know
your Love would enjoy.

∞ 211 ∞

LOVE ON THE TUBE

Rent a romantic movie for the two of you to watch together.
Take it a step further and buy popcorn and hotdogs to
accompany the show.

∞ 212 ∞

GETTING IN THE KNOW

Ask your Love to spend an evening teaching you all about
something your Love is interested in, yet you know little
about.

❧ 213 ❧

BY SPECIAL INVITATION

If the two of you are married, take your wedding invitation,
adorn it with dried flowers or lace, or decoupage it, then put
it in a frame.

❧ 214 ❧

HUNTING SEASON

Plant small gifts (perfume/cologne, CDs, candy, golf balls,
pantyhose, etc.) all around your Love's home. Each should
have a clue as to where to find the next. You are the final
clue and your gift is…well…up to you.

❧ 215 ❧

CUSTOM CASSETTE

Make a cassette tape of songs that have special meaning to
the two of you. Between songs, you can have personal
commentary.

∞ 216 ∞

SURPRISE MAIL
For no special reason, shop for a fun card and send it to your
Love in the mail.

∞ 217 ∞

TEMPORARY INSANITY
Buy some temporary tattoos. You can either put them on your
Love, or put them on yourself and let your Love search to
find them.

∞ 218 ∞

FROM A DISTANCE
If your relationship is one of long distance, rent a video
camera for a day and have a friend film your typical day.
Pepper the background with pictures or items owned by your
Love for amusement.

∽ 219 ∽

LIVE PERFORMANCE

Buy two concert tickets to see your Love's favorite performer
the next time he or she is performing nearby.

∽ 220 ∽

MAKESHIFT CHARIOT

Rent a carriage or turn your car into a chariot. Take your
Love for a ride on the next starry night.

∽ 221 ∽

BAKE-OFF

Everyone loves to come home to the smell of something
baking. Bake cookies or a cake and have icing and tools ready
for the two of you to decorate. Have à la mode capability
waiting in the freezer.

∽ 222 ∽

SOCK IT TO 'EM

Your love can never have enough socks. Buy a fun pair, then hide them in the bottom of your Love's sock drawer to be discovered when your Love is almost out of clean pairs. If this was a success, try the same concept with underwear.

∽ 223 ∽

POLITICAL CONTRIBUTION

Contribute to your Love's cause by giving an afternoon to working for some cause your Love supports and really cares about.

∽ 224 ∽

ON STAGE

Many theaters will rent out their stages. As a gift, invite your Love to the theater where you are the one-person show. It can be a comedy, monologue, or a reading of prose.

∞ 225 ∞

WARM AND STICKY
All the fixings for making S'mores—Hershey's® chocolate bars, graham crackers, marshmallows, marshmallow roasting sticks, and a fire.

∞ 226 ∞

RELATIONSHIP INPUT
Have family and friends write letters about how they view your relationship. Put the letters in a scrapbook and give it to your love.

∞ 227 ∞

COURTIN' & KISSIN'
There are two great books out entitled *365 Ways to Kiss your Love* and *365 Ways to Date your Love*. They come pre-wrapped with a bow around them and make a great gift. By the way, the author is…well, me.

∞ 228 ∞

A BIT OF BUBBLY

A bottle of champagne and two lovely champagne flutes. You could turn this into a tradition. It's a great way to add to your crystal collection.

∞ 229 ∞

WORTH A THOUSAND WORDS

Find the oldest possible photo of the two of you together and have it enlarged. Place it over your Love's bathroom mirror so that it is the first thing seen in the morning.

∞ 230 ∞

PHOTO FATALITIES

We all have bad pictures of ourselves. Find several that your Love has not yet seen, make color copies, then plant them in places so your Love will find them throughout the day. Some locations include: wallet, car seat, desk drawer, pillow, pockets, gloves, book.

∞ 231 ∞

SCRAPS OF LOVE

Create a scrapbook of your relationship. Include meaningful memorabilia such as ticket stubs, matchbooks, napkins, menus, maps, postcards, invitations, and photos. Present it as dessert at a special dinner.

∞ 232 ∞

SUNNY AND SICK

On the next beautiful, sunny day, call in sick and treat your Love to a "Ferris Bueller's Day Off." Watch a parade, go to a museum, have lunch at a fancy restaurant.

∞ 233 ∞

CHILDHOOD READ

Ask your Love's parents or siblings for the title of your Love's favorite book as a child. If your Love doesn't have the book, hunt it down.

∞ 234 ∞

PHOTO-OP

Grab your camera and find some place where there are a lot
of people around who you can ask to take your picture. Your
poses can be silly, symbolic, or sentimental. Give the best
shots to your Love.

∞ 235 ∞

PAMPERED

Treat your Love to a day at a spa. If you can't afford to send
your Love to one, turn your home into one. Give a facial,
shampoo, manicure, and pedicure. Conclude with a massage
where you take romantic license and kiss each toe and finger.

∞ 236 ∞

HEART-FELT BREAKFAST

A heart-shaped breakfast. Using a heart-shaped cookie cutter,
cut pieces of English, muffins, toast, butter, sausages, eggs,
pancakes or French toast. Have strawberries, powdered sugar,
and whipped cream as condiments.

∞ 237 ∞

MOUSING AROUND

Customize a computer mouse pad for your Love. Draw on it with markers or paint with fingernail polish. Place it under the mouse.

∞ 238 ∞

SENTIMENTAL SCENT

Next time your Love goes on a trip, wrap one of your pieces of clothing that has your scent on it with a ribbon and put it in your Love's suitcase to find when unpacking. Perhaps include a sweet note as well.

∞ 239 ∞

ENDEARING ENGRAVING

Have something out of the ordinary engraved on something out of the ordinary. It could be a piece of silverware engraved with a special date, a garden tool engraved with a poem, a can of your Love's favorite food engraved with a message.

❧ 240 ❧

TOASTY TOES

A hot water bottle to fill and place at the foot of your Love's bed on the next chilly night.

❧ 241 ❧

SPRAY IT, DON'T SAY IT.

A set of squirt guns.

❧ 242 ❧

LIST OF FAVORITES

Make a list titled, "My Love's Favorites." On the list put the phone numbers and names of favorite restaurants, gift stores, bookstores, florists, sporting goods stores, lingerie stores, kitchen stores, bath shops, hotels, and anything else. Give the list to your love to verify that you've made the right selections. Now tell your Love you will keep it and refer to it for future gifts.

∞ 243 ∞

THANK-YOU NOTE

Write your Love a thank-you note for some of the things that
make you love your Love so much.

∞ 244 ∞

COUPLE'S MAIL BOX

Make an indoor mail box with his-and-hers doors and flags
that raise and lower. Use it as a vehicle to deliver gifts and
notes to each other.

∞ 245 ∞

SURPRISE DINNER CERTIFICATE

A custom-made certificate good for one dinner at an
undisclosed location. On the night of redemption, set out the
proper clothes and shoes for your Love, put paste on your
Love's toothbrush, draw a bath, and pick the appropriate
fragrance.

∞ 246 ∞

POTPOURRI TAKEOUT

Pick up your Love's favorite dishes from all your Love's
favorite restaurants and bring them home for a special dinner.

∞ 247 ∞

CHALKY

Chalk a big heart shape in the driveway or on the front door
with "I Love You" written in the middle.

∞ 248 ∞

PET PASSPORT

Yes, you can actually get one for your Love's beloved pet. Call
1-800-345-VETS.

∞ 249 ∞

GONE WITH THE WIND

A set of wind chimes. Everyone loves the sound.

∞ 250 ∞

CALL OF THE WILD

Most zoos have an "adoption" program where you can make a
donation in your Love's name and your Love receives
"adoption" papers for one of the zoo's animals for the year.
It's a wild gift.

∞ 251 ∞

CHOCOLATE LOVER

If a real chocophile, your Love will surely enjoy receiving *The
Chocolatier Magazine*. Delivered bi-monthly, it costs $24. Call
(815) 734-1109 for more details.

∞ 252 ∞

HOT NUMBER

A pair of kitchen mitts to be given to your Love after a
romantic night. The note attached should read either "You
were too hot to handle" or "Wear these; I'm going to be too
hot to handle."

❧ 253 ❧

PERFECT PRESCRIPTION

Find some prescription bottles and replace the labels with prescriptions for love. How about "Loveomiacin," or "Smoochafed." Include dosage and the doctor prescribing. Of course the contents are M&Ms, jelly beans, or cinnamon candies. Get really carried away and fill your Love's entire medicine cabinet.

❧ 254 ❧

BUMPER CAR

Have a custom bumper sticker made and put on your Love's car.

❧ 255 ❧

BALLOONAGRAMS

Have several dozen balloons blown up with messages to your Love inside. Give your Love a pin with a ribbon tied around it, then lead your Love to the balloon pile.

∾ 256 ∾

MORNING DELIGHT

Have a warm towel from the dryer waiting after your Love's
morning shower, set out pills/vitamins, pour a morning drink,
have a newspaper ready, and have breakfast waiting, too.
Most importantly, stay out of the way while your Love is
getting ready.

∾ 257 ∾

"I DO" CAKE

Have a small wedding cake made. Tell your Love you became
inspired while thinking of your wedding. If the two of you
aren't married, this may be a good way to pop the question.

∾ 258 ∾

SCRIBBLE, SCRABBLE®

Buy a Scrabble® game for your Love, but not for playing.
Instead leave it out so you can leave messages for your Love.
Instruct your Love to scramble the letters after reading it.
That way you'll know the message was received.

∞ 259 ∞

BEDDY-BYE

Turn down your Love's bed, place a treat on the pillow,
toothpaste on the brush, lay out night clothes and slippers,
and put a glass of water on the nightstand. When your Love
is ready for bed, tuck your Love in, place a kiss on the
forehead, and turn out the lights.

∞ 260 ∞

COOL BOARD

Buy a chalkboard or writing board for your Love's refrigerator.
Guaranteed to increase communication.

∞ 261 ∞

CALENDAR LOVE

Make a custom calendar for your Love. Find twelve
photographs of yourself, blow them up, and then glue them to
a calendar. Title it "Your Calendar Boy (or Girl)."

∞ 262 ∞

DOWN FOR THE COUNT
You've heard of breakfast in bed. Well, surprise your Love
with dinner in bed.

∞ 263 ∞

PILLOW TALK
Have a pillow made with a special message on it.

∞ 264 ∞

LOVING CUP
A very special cup for your Love to have at work or home to
drink coffee out of.

∞ 265 ∞

PRECIOUS TOOTSIES
Find an unusual and very special pair of slippers for your
Love.

∞ 266 ∞

SAFE KEEPING

Does your Love have the necessary safety items in the event of a fire? If not, buy your Love a smoke detector, fire extinguisher, or safety ladder. Show you really care about your Love's safety.

∞ 267 ∞

GREAT HANG-UPS

Make your Love a picture hanging kit. Things such as a hammer, various sizes of hooks, hanging wire, all organized in a container. Your Love will have everything needed to display a new piece of artwork on the wall.

∞ 268 ∞

TABLE TOPPINGS

Buy your Love a set of table accessories for two. Some ideas include napkins, tablecloth, placemats, candlesticks, napkin rings, centerpiece, and seat cushions.

❧ 269 ❧

LESSON IN LOVE

Has your Love ever wanted to learn to rollerblade? Dance the foxtrot? Make sushi? Give the gift of knowledge with a paid-for lesson from an expert.

❧ 270 ❧

SKIP PACK

A gift box of great skipping rocks. Promise to take your Love to a body of water to use them on.

❧ 271 ❧

MASQUERADE

A costume with a mapped-out adventure enclosed.

❧ 272 ❧

RENT TO OWN

Bikes, in-line skates, windsurfers, or Harley-Davidsons: Rent a pair for the day and enjoy yourselves.

∽ 273 ∽

MARRIAGE VOWS

A framed copy of your wedding vows. Or, write your own
vows then give them to your Love.

∽ 274 ∽

PICK OF THE VINE

A bottle of wine from the year of your Love's birth, or of the
year that you first met.

∽ 275 ∽

BLOOMING THINGS

Flowers that have been individually picked in the wild or
individually selected and delivered by you.

∽ 276 ∽

DOWN UNDER

A piece of special underwear for your Love. Men have nice
underwear selections, too.

∽ 277 ∽

PERPETUAL BLOOM

Bring home one beautiful flower every day for your Love and
place them one at a time in a vase. As one flower fades, the
new one for the day will take its place. You can even get
more fancy and include a card or note with each flower.

∽ 278 ∽

GO DRY OFF

A special towel or robe for your Love to use after a shower or
bath. It could be an extra soft, fluffy towel, or one of those
towels that dries hair quickly. The robe could have a hood to
keep your Love's head warm, or Velcro® closings.

∽ 279 ∽

HOLIDAY TREAT

Next holiday, treat your Love to a holiday theme gift. It
could be a holiday cake, holiday tie or earrings, or a holiday
decoration for your Love's desk. Consider having it delivered.

❧ 280 ❧

SPECIAL POP

A can full of special gourmet popcorn you know your Love would like. Have two movie tickets to the film your Love wants to see attached.

❧ 281 ❧

GET ORGANIZED

Organize that project your Love has never gotten around to organizing. It could be labeling the VCR tapes, organizing your Love's book collection, alphabetizing CDs, spicing up the spice rack, chronologizing photographs, etc.

❧ 282 ❧

GIFT BOX

A specially decorated box to put your Love's treasures in or to have around to put a present in the next time you get one for your Love.

∽ 283 ∽

GROCERY SPREE

If you think about it, a grocery store has all the things your
Love loves. Do the grocery shopping for your Love and bring
back all the things your Love loves to eat and drink.

∽ 284 ∽

SLICE OF LIFE

Make your Love a homemade pie from scratch (including the
crust). Use your Love's favorite ingredients and cut a special
message out on the top, or sprinkle a message in cinnamon.

∽ 285 ∽

COOKIES WITH A MESSAGE

Make cookies the shapes of letters that spell out a special
message. Give the cookies to your love and have your Love
unscramble them. Maybe include some clues if your Love is
having trouble.

❦ 286 ❦

FANCY FEATHER
A fabulous feather for tickling or caressing.

❦ 287 ❦

GET LUCKY
A collection of lucky charms: four-leaf clover, rabbit's foot,
Indian head penny, and anything else lucky you can find.

❦ 288 ❦

CROWNING GLORY
A beautifully made crown or tiara to be presented on a satin
pillow to your king or queen.

❦ 289 ❦

FRIENDLY LUNCH
Arrange for your Love to have lunch with a friend who hasn't
been seen in quite a while. You could make it a bigger surprise
by paying to have a friend flown in from out of town.

∞ 290 ∞

TRAY CHIC
A bed tray, linens, and a certificate for breakfast in bed for an
entire week.

∞ 291 ∞

CHECK REFERENCES
There are many reference books available today. Perhaps
there's one your Love would enjoy. For example, there's a
reference book listing every public golf course in America, a
book listing all the mail-order resources for gardeners, a
manual of all outlet malls in America. Surely there is one
relating to a sport, hobby, or career that your Love would like.

∞ 292 ∞

PERSONAL PROTECTION
What better way to show your Love you care than by giving
something for protection. A can of mace, a car alarm, a
mobile phone, a brighter porch light, a dog, or a reflective
vest for running or walking at night.

∞ 293 ∞

POETIC VERSE

A book of poems with earmarked pages that lead your Love
to those poems which best express your feelings.

∞ 294 ∞

TIPTOEING THROUGH TULIPS

A ukulele with a book teaching your Love how to play it.

∞ 295 ∞

CUSTOM-MAID

Hire a maid to clean your Love's home.

∞ 296 ∞

WALL TO WALL

Have your Love's carpeting and rugs cleaned by an expert.

∞ 297 ∞

GREAT RETURN

The ventilation system in a home can trap germs and spread dust. Have your Love's return vents professionally cleaned.

∞ 298 ∞

WINDOWS OF OPPORTUNITY

Wash all the windows in your Love's house.

∞ 299 ∞

FUN FUNNIES

Buy your Love a comic book collection of the heroes and characters your Love enjoyed as a child.

∞ 300 ∞

LEISURE WEAR

Buy your Love a comfortable outfit to enjoy wearing around the house. Consider personalizing it with a monogram and include something comfortable for your Love's feet, too.

∞ 301 ∞

I SCREAM, YOU SCREAM

Make homemade ice cream in your Love's favorite flavor.

∞ 302 ∞

A MAP OF MY HEART

That's the title of your collage. Now, find things you feel
strongly about and create a collage. For example, stamps if
you're a stamp collector, a Snickers wrapper if that's your
favorite snack, the face of a watch if you're a time freak, a
drawing of shoes if you are the next potential Imelda Marcos.

∞ 303 ∞

ALWAYS IN CONTROL

There is nothing more frustrating than not having batteries
around when your remote control goes out or the garage door
opener quits. Buy your Love a collection of batteries. Maybe
even a battery charger.

∽ 304 ∽

TOUCH-UP

Look around your Love's home. Surely there are nicks in the paint on the baseboards, around cabinet edges, on the doors. Surprise your Love with a paint touch-up.

∽ 305 ∽

HIGH POLISH

Silver and brass need constant attention. You'll be a guaranteed hero when your Love discovers you've polished all the silver and brass items.

∽ 306 ∽

RULES OF ENGAGEMENT

Write up the rules which you agree to follow the next time you have an argument. For example, "I won't give you the silent treatment." "I promise to listen before speaking." "I promise to not let the sun go down on my anger." Maybe your Love will be inspired to make a separate list.

∞ 307 ∞

MONTHLY ACCOUNTING
Prepare your Love's end-of-month bills so all that has to be done is the signing of the checks.

∞ 308 ∞

BALANCING ACT
Balance your Love's checkbook as soon as the statement arrives. Make sure this is a loving act and not an inquisition.

∞ 309 ∞

CHILDLIKE
If you have children, great, if not, round up a couple to make a choir. Have them serenade your Love with a favorite song.

∞ 310 ∞

CHAUFFEUR
Offer to act as your Love's chauffeur the next time your Love needs to go somewhere.

∞ 311 ∞

SERVICE WITH A SMILE

Take your Love's car in and then pick it up the next time it needs service.

∞ 312 ∞

BADGE OF HONOR

Make a button for your Love that reads: "My Love wants everyone to know I'm the best."

∞ 313 ∞

NIGHTWEAR

Buy both of you something new to go to bed in.

∞ 314 ∞

SPECIAL WISH

A wishbone, dried, tied with a ribbon and placed in a box. It is for your Love to bring out next time he or she wants you to help make a wish come true.

∞ 315 ∞

THIS LITTLE PIGGY

Buy a piggy bank for your Love. Tell your Love all your loose change will go into it to help buy them a ticket to see a long-distance friend or family member.

∞ 316 ∞

BABY FACE

Find a baby picture of each of you and have them framed. If you have children, add their baby pictures to the collection. Baby pictures of the pets can be fun, too.

∞ 317 ∞

HONORABLE MENTION

Gather up all your Love's certificates of achievement, trophies, ribbons, and anything else that shows accomplishments. Now frame what you can, and then find a place to display them. What better way to show how proud you are of your Love.

❧ 318 ❧

BACK-SCRATCH FEVER
Who doesn't love a back scratch? Offer one to your Love.

❧ 319 ❧

WALL ALBUM
Find pictures of your Love's family and have them framed. Hang them all together on a wall and tell your Love it's a family wall album.

❧ 320 ❧

BETWEEN THE SLICES
Buy your Love all the ingredients to make a favorite sandwich. Don't forget to buy the right spreads as well as a favorite bread.

❧ 321 ❧

SWEET SOUNDS
A stereo system for your Love's bedroom.

❧ 322 ❧

PERKY MORNING
Buy a small electric coffee machine and mug to put in your
Love's bedroom for an early morning cup of coffee.

❧ 323 ❧

SECOND TO NONE
Pay to have a second phone line brought into your Love's
home. The new line is just for the two of you. When it rings,
your Love will know it's you.

❧ 324 ❧

ARTSY IDEA
Buy your Love a set of body paints.

❧ 325 ❧

COLLECTOR'S EDITION
Purchase an addition to whatever your Love collects.

∞ 326 ∞

PACK IT IN

Next time your Love is leaving on a trip without you, set up
the suitcase and do some preliminary packing. Put some
sweet reminders of you to find when your Love unpacks.

∞ 327 ∞

A BROWNING IDEA

Elizabeth Barrett Browning had a great idea. Make a scroll,
and title it "How do I love thee? Let me count the ways…"
Now make a list (try for a hundred ways). When you are
finished, roll it up and wrap a ribbon around it.

∞ 328 ∞

A GALA EVENT

Throw a gala in your Loved one's honor. Include a
coronation ceremony.

⊙ 329 ⊙

SPECIAL GROOMING
Have your Love's pet groomed.

⊙ 330 ⊙

POINTED PILLOW
Needlepoint one of those small message pillows to give to your Love. A note to men: You guys can do this. It's simple and isn't that time-consuming.

⊙ 331 ⊙

VOICE MAIL
Set your Love up with a personal voice mail. Be the first to leave a message on it.

⊙ 332 ⊙

SOCK IT AWAY
Organize your Love's sock drawer. Sort out the ones that are getting thin or have holes and replace them with new ones.

∞ 333 ∞

JACK IT UP
Give your Love a little gift wrapped inside a box of Cracker Jacks.®

∞ 334 ∞

WAITING TO EXHALE
Buy your Love a harmonica. Present it after you have performed your Love's favorite song on it.

∞ 335 ∞

SEE THROUGH
Have a stained glass window made for your Love. Better yet, take a class and make it for your Love.

∞ 336 ∞

SNAP! CRACKLE! POP!
Put on a fireworks display in honor of your Love.

∞ 337 ∞

LOOSE CHANGE

Collect all your Love's loose change, sort it, then put it in rolls for your Love to cash at the bank.

∞ 338 ∞

A NEW CALLING

Pay to have your Love's phone service enhanced for a year. Give your Love Caller ID, call blocking, phone mailbox, and any other feature you think your Love would like.

∞ 339 ∞

A B_{12} C

Go to a vitamin store and research what vitamins and minerals your Love could benefit from taking. Present them to your Love in a box with a bottle of water, glass for drinking and a pill carrying case.

❧ 340 ❧

IMMORTALIZE
Bronze your Love's baby shoes. If this has already been done, then bronze your Love's favorite food.

❧ 341 ❧

FOUND IDENTITY
Have one of those old-fashioned identity bracelets made for your Love.

❧ 342 ❧

GOOD INSURANCE
Put your Love's name on your life insurance policy.

❧ 343 ❧

SPECIAL MUSIC
A music box that plays your Love's favorite song.

∞ 344 ∞

RECIPE FOR SUCCESS

Organize all your Love's recipes. Add any recipes you have
that you know your Love would like as well. Call family
members and get the recipes to your Love's favorite dishes. If
your Love has no recipes, start a collection.

∞ 345 ∞

SPIN DOCTOR

A beautiful empty bottle with a note explaining it is your
Love's official bottle for playing spin the bottle, any time.

∞ 346 ∞

SWINGER

A porch swing for your Love and you.

∞ 347 ∞

SWEET-TOOTH MONTH

Treat your Love to homemade desserts for an entire month.

∞ 348 ∞

SOUTH OF THE BORDER

Give your Love a piñata. Hang it and have your Love break
it open with a stick. Have it filled with your Love's favorite
candy and a special gift.

∞ 349 ∞

A LINE IN TIME

Create a timeline of your Love's life. It can be your Love's
entire life or the time of your life together. Interview friends
and family members to discover milestones. Write notations
along the line that are sentimental, funny, and serious. Roll it
up into a scroll and wrap it with a ribbon.

∞ 350 ∞

FROM A TO Z

Surprise your Love with twenty-six little gifts, each beginning
with a different letter of the alphabet. For example, a can of
Apple juice, a box of Bon Bons, a Card, etc.

∞ 351 ∞

PERSONAL SHOPPER
Do the shopping for your Love. It could be your Love's
Christmas shopping, grocery shopping, or gift shopping.

∞ 352 ∞

DONATION
Donate blood in your Love's name.

∞ 353 ∞

CHARGE IT
Open a charge account for your Love at a favorite store with
a credit balance already on it.

∞ 354 ∞

PERSONAL DECK
Custom-made playing cards. They can be hand drawn or a
collection of 52 photographs. Be as conservative or
outrageous as you like.

∞ 355 ∞

DAISY PICKS

Give your Love a bouquet of daisies to perform the daisy test on. You know, "She/He loves me, she/he loves me not." Of course, you have checked each daisy to assure success.

∞ 356 ∞

IN THE CARDS

Save up all the cards your Love has given you, then have them framed or turned into a collage, and hang them on a special wall.

∞ 357 ∞

FRAME IT

A picture of yourself, which your Love has never seen, in a special frame.

∞ 358 ∞

MAP IT OUT

Make a road map that represents your relationship and show where you think the two of you are going.

∞ 359 ∞

COUNT THE WAYS

Write down all the reasons you fell in Love with your Love on individual cards. Place the cards in surprising places for your Love to find.

∞ 360 ∞

TOOL OF THE TRADE

A cooking utensil, gardening tool, or hobby tool to make your Love's chore a little easier.

∞ 361 ∞

SIGN HERE

Get the autograph of one of your Love's heroes.

✆ 362 ✆

CHAIN OF HEARTS
Make a paper heart chain, then write little notes and
messages on each heart.

✆ 363 ✆

FAIRY TALE
A magic wand wrapped with a bow and a note saying you will
always try to make your Love's wishes come true.

✆ 364 ✆

SEEMS FISHY
Buy a pair of goldfish in a bowl to give your Love. Name
them after each of you.

✆ 365 ✆

CAMPY IDEA
Build a campfire pit outside for you and your Love to snuggle
around and toast marshmallows.